Christmas in
GREECE

Kinisis Theotokov Church greets the sunrise in Santorini, Thira, in the Cyclades Islands.

Christmas in
GREECE

*Christmas Around the World
from World Book*

World Book, Inc.
a Scott Fetzer company
Chicago

Staff

President
Robert C. Martin

Editorial

Managing Editor
Maureen Mostyn Liebenson

Senior Editor
Shawn Brennan

Writer
Ellen Hughes

Permissions Editor
Janet T. Peterson

Executive Director, Product
Development and Research Services
Paul A. Kobasa

Head, Indexing Services
David Pofelski

Staff Indexer
Tina Trettin

Art

Executive Director
Roberta Dimmer

Art Director
Wilma Stevens

Designer
Don Di Sante

Senior Photographs Editor
Sandra Dyrlund

Photographs Editor
Carol Parden

Product Production

Manufacturing Manager
Barbara Podczerwinski

Manufacturing Assistant Manager
Valerie Piarowski

Senior Production Manager
Madelyn Underwood

Proofreaders
Anne Dillon
Chad Rubel

Text Processing
Gwendolyn Johnson

World Book wishes to thank the following individuals for their contributions to *Christmas in Greece*: Lia Constantinides, Bradley Hannan, Christine Kintonis, Connie Mourtoupalas, Jeanne Johnson, and Katie Sharp.

World Book, Inc.
233 N. Michigan Avenue
Chicago, IL 60601

For information on other World Book products, call
1-800-WORLDBK (967-5325), or visit our Web site at
www.worldbook.com

ISBN 0-7166-0859-6
Library of Congress Catalog Card No. 00-105875

Printed in the United States of America
by The HF Group LLC, North Manchester, Indiana
6th printing June 2011

Contents

Greek Traditions Come Alive at Christmas

In Greece, Christmas happens in the heart and in the home. Christmas touches the very essence of the powerful Greek Orthodox religion with its ancient and deeply spiritual images and rituals. Christmas celebrations—in downtown Athens, on the Greek islands, or in rocky mountainside villages—center where all Greek life centers: at home, in the loving company of family and friends.

The history of Greece is a history of a people. It is a rich history not of a land, but of a nation. The Greek idea of nationality is governed by language, religion, descent, and customs. Its early history is one of internal struggle from the Mycenaean and Minoan cultures of the Bronze Age to the competing city-states that emerged in the 1st millennium B.C. Yet despite these struggles, Greece maintained its unique identity and culture while sharing with the world its magnificent achievements in government, science, philosophy, and the arts that still influence our lives today.

Ancient Greece was the birthplace of Western civilization about 2,500 years ago. Greek civilization developed chiefly in small city-states. A city-state consisted of a city or town and the surrounding villages and farmland. The Greek city-states were fiercely independent and often quarreled among themselves. But their small size and constant rivalry had certain advantages. Citizens of a city-state were strongly patriotic, and many citizens took part in public affairs. The most advanced city-states established the world's first democratic governments. The best-known city-states were Athens and Sparta.

The ancient Greek city-states never became united into a nation. However, a common language, religion, and culture bound the people together. The Greeks called themselves *Hellenes* and their land *Hellas*. They thought of themselves as different from all other peoples, whom they called *barbarians*.

The ancient Greeks prized their freedom and way of life. This way of life stressed importance of the individual and encouraged creative thought. Greek thinkers laid the foundations of science and philosophy by seeking logical explanations for what happened in the world around them. Greek writers created new forms of expression, which explored human personalities and emotions. Greek civilization reached its height in Athens during the mid-400's B.C., a period of outstanding achievement known as the Golden Age.

The ancient Greeks believed that certain deities (gods and goddesses) watched over them and directed daily events. Families tried to please household deities with offerings and ceremonies. Each city-state honored one or more deities as protectors of the community and held annual festivals in their honor.

Lygabetus Hill rises behind a simple but beautiful Greek Orthodox church. About 98 percent of Greece's people are Greek Orthodox, the nation's official religion.

The Greek flag has a white cross symbolizing the Greek Orthodox religion. The blue stripes represent the sea and sky. The white stripes stand for the purity of the struggle for independence.

The Greeks believed that their deities could foretell the future. People flocked to shrines called *oracles* to consult priests and priestesses. Deities supposedly spoke through the priests and priestesses to answer questions and reveal the future.

There is much of the spirit of ancient Greece alive in the Greeks of today. Religious devotion and faith, family, and identity are still important to most Greeks.

The Christmas holiday time in Greece is a time when the flames of faith, family, and identity burn especially bright. Customs of the ancient Greeks are not unlike the traditions Greeks celebrate during the Christmas holiday season today.

Just as the ancient Greeks looked to deities for protection and paid homage to them with annual festivals, today Greeks

honor Saints Basil and Nicholas during the Christmas season
with feast days and celebrations. Modern Greeks behold the
mystical power of saints and the Nativity in religious icons in
churches and in the *ikonostàsi*, or home altar. The ancient Greeks
looked to deities, priests, and oracles to reveal the future.
Today's Greeks observe colorful and whimsical traditions to
glimpse into the future on New Year's Eve and New Year's Day,
from *kálanda* singers bringing good luck to your doorstep with
carols, to getting the lucky coin hidden in the *Vasilopita*, or St.
Basil's bread.

In many regions, Christmastime in Greece is a solemn,
religious time. But it is also a special time of great beauty and
meaning as Greek hearts rejoice and celebrate their faith,
history, culture, and identity with family and friends.

**Athens, Greece's
capital and largest
city, contains many
reminders of ancient
Greek civilizations,
such as the Temple
of Poseidon in the
region of Attica.**

Hearts Prepare for Christmas

The weeks before Christmas in Greece are a time of anticipation and intense preparation. In other countries, the approach of Christmas finds people busy buying presents, decorating, and gathering for Christmas parties. In Greece, the focus is different. Here people are devoted to preparing their hearts to receive the newborn Christ.

The Greek Orthodox Church is a central force in the life of Greece, where it is the state religion. Nearly the entire population is Greek Orthodox. The rituals and traditions of the church are woven deeply into everyday life. This is a religion of incredible beauty, of deeply rewarding spirituality, and of strict traditions. All of this is readily apparent in the Greek celebration of Christmas.

Christmas Lent is a solemn 40-day period of fasting and reflection. It begins November 15 and continues until Christmas Eve. During this time, devout Greeks focus on preparing themselves spiritually for the arrival of the Christ Child.

For the Greek Orthodox, this is not a time for parties or merrymaking. Instead, it is a time for fasting, confession, and deep reflection. People attend church services, make confessions, and take Communion as they prepare. The Christmas Lent fast is strictly observed. It requires abstinence from all meat, milk products, and other rich foods.

Fasting

Fasting is an essential component of Greek Orthodox religious life. Though the focus is on dietary restrictions, fasting in the Greek Orthodox religion is much more. To the devout, fasting is a total body-and-mind experience to purify the body and the soul. To fast means to demonstrate self-control over temptations, sins, unkind feelings, and material desires.

As one Orthodox hymn says, fasting is "the casting off of evil, the bridling of the tongue, the cutting off of anger, the cessation of lusts, evil talking, lies, and cursings."

In the Greek Orthodox religion, followers fast every Wednesday and Friday throughout the year, on a number of special fast days, and during four major lents: the 49-day Great Lent before Easter; Holy Apostles' Lent (beginning the Monday after the week following Pentecost, and ending the eve of June 28); the Dormition (ascension into heaven) of the Mother of God Lent (August 1-14); and the 40-day Christmas Lent.

A fast can be designated formal, *tessarakosti*, or informal. As the lenten period begins, people greet each other with *"Kalí Sarakostí,"* or "Good Lent."

Dietary restrictions vary from fast to fast and from family to family. Most extreme is a severe fast, which means no eating or

The Dodecameron is a time when light has great meaning. Following pre-Christian custom, the 12 days are a symbolic time of moving from the dark days to a return of the light. Both ancient and Christian symbols make this a time of hope, a time when good triumphs over evil and the future looks bright.

drinking at all. Less severe is a strict fast, in which certain foods and activities are prohibited. Least restrictive is a moderate fast. Here, what you eat and do are determined by your own family customs.

Christmas Lent in Greece is a strict fast. Strict fasting is called *xeropháyi*, which translates as "dry eating." A strict fast means no meat, fish with a backbone, cheese, milk, butter, eggs, lard, olive oil, or alcohol other than a little wine. You may eat shellfish, fruit, vegetables, bread, legumes, and vegetable oil. By doing without rich earthly delights in the weeks leading up to Christmas, Greeks prepare their body and mind to welcome Christ.

For children, Christmas Lent is not necessarily a hardship. Many feel excited to be doing something different and important, and they have a Christmas banquet to look forward to. Meanwhile, plenty of fresh vegetables and potatoes will be presented in many different ways by clever cooks.

> ## To the devout, fasting is a total body-and-mind experience to purify the body and the soul.

What matters above all during a fast is a person's attitude. The purpose of the fast is destroyed if people boast about it or show their suffering. Rather, they should be in a calm and happy state, ready to receive God. In keeping with this idea, the church asks that people take no food or water for at least six hours before attending church services.

Christmas Lent ends with a fast-breaking feast on Christmas Day. Then a period of good eating and merrymaking begins. In fact, the days between December 25 and January 4, including Wednesdays and Fridays, are officially declared fast-free.

Preparing for a Feast

The long, solemn vigil of the fast makes the coming joyful event of Christmas seem all the more wondrous. As the lenten period stretches on, anticipation builds toward the sumptuous Christmas feast. As Christmas draws nearer, women begin to ready the ingredients for the Christmas feast and for parties in the days ahead.

For Greek children, there is work to be done now, but it is work they are glad to do. Women find special jobs for their small helpers. Figs and other fruits must be gathered and spread out on rooftops to dry. Nuts must be gathered, shelled, and

A modern market in Athens displays some of the items a clever cook may use to prepare meals during Christmas Lent fasting days.

blanched. Then the dried fruits and nuts must be chopped or finely ground and made ready to be mixed into all kinds of delicate Christmas pastries and sumptuous cakes. Pastries like *baklavá*, made of many layers of phíllo pastry and finely ground walnuts and almonds, require hours of work to make.

The long fast is about to be broken with great feasting. It is the tradition in some parts of the Greek countryside for the family to slaughter a pig on Christmas Eve day for Christmas Day dinner and the following holiday period.

On Christmas Eve, preparation of the family Christmas feast is the focus of all activity at home. The *Christopsomo*, or Christmas bread, is baked. The table is set for the coming dinner, including a place set for St. Basil, one of the most revered saints in the Greek Orthodox religion.

After everything is set, the family heads to church to take Communion and attend the Liturgy of St. Basil the Great and the Glorification of Christ. This liturgy is a meaningful and popular time to take Communion because it commemorates when Christ and His disciples shared the Last Supper. A lighted candle is placed in the center of the church, symbolizing the light of Christ in the world.

Like Christian countries everywhere, Greece lights up the dark winter skies at Christmas.

Heading home afterward with lighted candles, some families now plan to end their fast by cutting the Christopsomo. Others save that moment for Christmas Day. Like Christian countries everywhere, Greece lights up the dark winter skies at Christmas. There are Christmas-light displays in Athens and other cities. Little villages string lights around squares and across streets. Still, there is no public celebration before Christmas Day.

Devotion in the Home: The Family Altar

Christmas decorating in Greek homes is likely to be something simple and meaningful. Christmas Lent centers on spiritual preparation, and so the focus is on the *ikonostási*, the family altar. In the Greek Orthodox home, this is a sacred place of worship in the physical center of the home. This is where family icons—small religious paintings—and other sacred religious items are kept. Here, family members pray and feel close to God.

St. Nicholas

Children everywhere love St. Nicholas. In many countries around the world, he's known as that jolly old fellow who arrives on Christmas Eve with his red suit, reindeer, and sack of toys. In other countries, St. Nicholas wears his bishop's robe and rides a donkey or walks into town on his feast day, December 6.

One thing is sure: St. Nicholas brings presents. He drops them down the chimney, throws them through a window, leaves them in a shoe or a stocking, or hands them out in person, depending on which house he's visiting in which country.

Not so in Greece. Here, St. Nicholas is no gift giver, but children love him just the same. In the Greek Orthodox religion, St. Nicholas is regarded as the patron saint of children, particularly orphans, and of sailors.

Rather than wearing a cozy red suit, in Greece, St. Nicholas is likely to be depicted draped in seaweed and dripping wet, fresh from rescuing sailors and ships in peril on the rough and stormy sea. No Greek ship would sail away from land without an icon of St. Nicholas aboard for protection.

The bishop of Myra in Turkey in the 300's, St. Nicholas withstood torture and imprisonment for his faith. Through it all, he kept a loving heart, especially toward children. He is admired for his faith and for his charity in bestowing gifts and kindnesses on poor children.

In Greece, St. Nicholas is not usually pictured as the jolly old elf in a red suit. Instead, his icon is more often found in an honored position in Greek Orthodox churches and homes.

St. Nicholas's icon is found in an honored position in Greek Orthodox churches and in many Greek homes. His feast day on December 6 is a happy occasion each year, with religious services and name day parties for the many children named in his honor.

Greek Orthodox priests honor St. Nicholas on his feast day.

The ikonostási is a wall cabinet or table beneath small shelves against an east wall of the home. That location allows people to face east when they pray. According to Orthodox beliefs, Christ will come from the East when he comes again.

For contemporary families, icons may simply be gathered in the corner of a room, usually a married couple's bedroom. There may be a frame containing the couple's wedding crowns (small wreaths worn on the head during the wedding ceremony), an icon next to the frame, and maybe a kandíli, a lamp that uses water and olive oil to burn, with a wick placed on a piece of cork for the flame.

Traditional items kept in the ikonostási include icons of Christ, the Virgin Mary, and the family's patron saint. A patron saint is a saint that protects and has special significance for a person, family, organization, city, or cause. For a family, it is often the saint for whom the head of the house is named.

There may also be icons of family members' individual saints or other beloved saints. There is always a cross, a prayer book, and a Bible. The *sfrayítha*, which is a seal used to print a religious design on communion bread, is kept in the ikonostási. So is a censer, which is a special container for incense, and always a light or candle.

In addition, the ikonostási holds important items from religious services throughout the year: the first piece of the *Vasilopita*, the New Year's bread; holy water from the Epiphany service; palms from Palm Sunday; holy oil; flowers from special services; and an Easter egg. Each of these holy items is kept in this place and disposed of only according to prescribed customs at special times.

In many homes, the light or candle is kept burning at all times as a reminder of the light of Christ and his presence in the home. In most homes, it would be kept burning constantly during the Christmas Lent and the following holiday season.

Use of incense varies, with the most devout carrying it from room to room twice a day as prayers are said. Incense is burned before a name day celebration (an annual celebration on the feast day of the saint for whom a person is named), a feast day, or other special occasion. Most people burn incense often during Christmas Lent especially because, according to Orthodox teaching, the prayers are carried directly to God on this sacred, scented smoke.

A lighted candle is placed in the center of the church, symbolizing the light of Christ in the world.

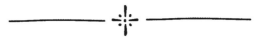

Glad Tidings

On the last day of Christmas Lent, the morning of Christmas Eve, the somber mood of waiting for Christmas is broken by the joyful sound of children singing. On this day, bands of children travel from house to house and store to store heralding the happy time to come. They sing the *kálanda*, Greek Christmas carols, and bring good luck to each home and each person they address. In return, people give them coins or treats.

This is the first of three days on which kálanda singers appear. They will come again on New Year's Eve and the Eve of Epiphany (January 6), each time singing ancient kálanda that address the day and bringing personal good wishes for all.

Icons

Greek Orthodox icons are mysterious and strangely beautiful religious pictures. Surreal, complex, and compelling icons presenting the nativity scene, the Virgin Mary and her newborn baby, and the saints draw believers into an intense and personal understanding of the miracle of Christmas. Icons are expressions of Greek Orthodox mysticism. It is said that to look intensely at an icon is to be transported into the presence of God and regard his holy realm. Never is this more manifest than at Christmas.

To a first-time viewer, the image of an icon may seem flat and two-dimensional. Expressions on the faces of the Virgin Mary, Christ, and the saints are somber. Their poses seem stiff and unnatural. Proportions may seem odd, with one figure much larger or smaller than others in the painting, and hands or heads much too big.

These qualities are intentional and express the meaning of an icon. Other Christian religions emphasize that God became human in the image of Christ. So they present realistic human images of Christ, the Virgin Mary, and the saints. The Greek Orthodox religion emphasizes instead the need for people to become like God. Images on icons are therefore purposefully unnatural, or "otherworldly." Saints pictured on icons are humans who have been transported to the spiritual world through their goodness. They have been transformed into divine beings. Saints portrayed on icons provide an image of divine grace, a role model to follow. Worshipers are encouraged to gaze at the image of an icon and let it take them closer to God.

In an icon of Christ, it is impossible to determine much about His appearance. He does not seem to belong to any specific race or nationality. A well-made icon of Jesus Christ is intended to transcend race, age, nationality, and time to present the essential Christ.

Icons: The Word of God

The word icon means "image." Icons are said to be "written" rather than drawn or painted. They are considered to be the living word of God translated into images.

Iconography is a sacred art. It is practiced by devout individuals trained by the church. Traditionally, icons were made by

Icons (top) are expressions of Greek Orthodox mysticism. They are considered to be the living word of God translated into images. An iconographer (left) must follow strict rules and traditions in making this sacred art.

monks in monasteries, using blessed brushes and paints. Today, icons are also made by individual artists elsewhere.

In making their sacred art, iconographers must follow strict rules and traditions. An iconographer's job is not to reveal a creative interpretation, but to carefully replicate the traditional pose of the subject. An icon always shows a saint in the same position. The hands are posed and the head tilted in exactly the same way every time.

For example, an icon of a saint may have very large eyes because they are the windows to his soul. An extremely high forehead leads viewers to the saint's spirit. One figure in a group scene may be much larger than all the others to show his or her importance.

Icons can be as big as a wall or ceiling fresco in a church or as small as a tiny piece of jewelry. The classic Greek Orthodox icon, on wood with egg tempera, has a deep, soft appearance. Icons may also be made on canvas, paper, or other materials. Sometimes precious metals are stamped into shape to cover all of an icon except the head or hands.

A Living Art

Today, the art of iconography is thriving in Greece and around the world. In Athens, the Pláka district is famous for its array of small artists' studios and shops offering icons of every size and type. Icons also may be purchased from a Greek Orthodox monastery.

An icon is not complete or sacred until it is blessed. Icons created at a monastery are blessed by their creators. An icon drawn by hand or purchased from a shop must be taken to a church for blessing. A priest places the icon on the altar for 40 days and says special prayers over it, thus giving it sacred value.

Venerating the icon

In the home, icons are traditionally kept in the ikonostási, or family altar. In addition to icons of Christ, the Virgin Mary, and the family's patron saint, icons of each family member's guardian saint and other beloved saints may be kept in the family altar. An icon of St. Basil, the beloved patron saint of children, is in a place of honor in most Greek homes.

Icons are very much a part of everyday living. They are found in many locations throughout the house. An icon of a child's patron saint may be in his or her bedroom. An icon of St. Demetrios the Great or St. George the Great, the patron saints of shepherds, might be in the main room of a shepherd's cottage. Icons of St. Joachim and St. Anna, the patron saints of pious parents, might be in the parents' bedroom. An icon of St. Irene, the patron saint of peace, might be near the front door. A small icon also is likely to be found on the dashboard of the family car, protecting passengers from "every evil end."

People venerate but do not worship icons. An icon is not a holy thing in itself, but rather a representation of a holy being or event. It is a visual image to help people connect to Christ or to a saint. Prayers before an icon are not directed to the icon but to the saint who is believed to be living in heaven and can help you.

To venerate an icon, worshipers light a candle, bow

> Icons of Christ, the Virgin Mary, the family's patron and guardian saints, and St. Basil are traditionally kept in the ikonostási, or family altar.

Christmas icons often depict the Nativity. All the earth and its creatures are shown offering something to welcome the Christ child.

The cave is dark, symbolizing the world before Christ came. Golden light illuminating the outside of the cave represents the light of Christ coming into the world.

According to Greek Orthodox teaching, everything on earth gave of itself to welcome the newborn Christ, just as people are still called to offer room in their hearts for Jesus.

The familiar Nativity scene figures are all pictured on the icon, each offering something to welcome the newborn Christ. The angels offer their songs, the shepherds offer their praise and adoration, and the wise men bear gifts after following a star to the Christ child. The animals in the cave give warmth with their bodies and their breath. The cave itself is the earth's offering of a sheltered place for the family.

On the icon, an elderly St. Joseph sits in the forefront, looking troubled. Bothering him is a wicked little man who seems to be wearing a disguise. This person represents the worries and confusion that plague Joseph, his wife, and this baby. After an angel comforts Joseph in a dream, he casts these tormenting thoughts aside.

In the forefront of the icon, there is a midwife washing and tending to the newborn baby Jesus. This is a reminder that this was a very human birth, that through Jesus, God became human.

before it while making the sign of the cross, and kiss the image. They might also leave a flower before an icon.

Christmas Icons

A beloved Greek Orthodox icon of the Nativity provides a beautiful visual representation of the birth of Christ. Here, many different passages from the Scriptures are presented in one rich symbolic image.

At the center of the image are the Virgin Mary and the baby Jesus, sheltered in a dark cave. According to Orthodox teaching, a cave rather than a wooden stable was the actual birthplace of Jesus. Caves are plentiful in the region of the Mediterranean and commonly were used to keep livestock at the time of Christ's birth.

Glad Tidings and Good Wishes

The sound of children singing is at the heart of the Greek Christmas celebration. On three very special days—Christmas Eve, New Year's Eve, and the Eve of the Epiphany, or *Theophania*—groups of children walk from house to house beginning early in the morning to sing the *kálanda*, ancient carols bringing good news and good wishes to the people they visit.

For every doorstep performance, the children are rewarded with treats or coins. The little bands may roam for hours, starting early and making as many stops as possible. In the city, the *kálanda* carolers may include shops, offices, or even crowded streetcars on their goodwill tours.

The kálanda, sung in celebration of the coming of Christ, of St. Basil, and of the new year ahead, have their origins in pagan customs for warding off evil and bringing good fortune. At various times in the past, Greek religious leaders have disapproved of the kálanda's pagan roots. For a long time now, though, the custom has been accepted as an essential part of Christmas holiday celebration everywhere in Greece.

Specifically, kálanda are Greek carols filled with wishes for the health and prosperity of a household in the year to come. Bands of children arrive at a house asking, *"Na ta poúme?"* or "May we sing for you?" The residents respond, *"Yia to kalo,"* welcoming them in "for luck."

The kálanda singers, traditionally all-boy groups, perform with their voices, accompanied by little metal triangles and small drums. Usually the songs are sweet and intended to sound like hymns sung by angel bands. But sometimes the singers may offer a boisterous or off-key rendition, intended to scare off any *kalikántzari*, mischievous Christmastime goblins, who may be lurking about. They begin by singing a traditional verse such as this, asking for permission to sing about the holiday to come:

> *I bid you good day, my lords,*
> *And with your permission*
> *Christ's divine birth*
> *I shall announce at your house.*
>
> *Christ is born*
> *In Bethlehem today,*
> *The Heavens are jubilant*
> *And the Universe is rejoicing.*
> *Praise and Good Wishes*

Next, the singers move on to individual verses praising the head of the household and each member of the family, as well as the house, farm, and any livestock.

A kálanda band in Athens sings carols and plays triangles and small drums.

The praise is extravagant; the wishes are for the very best. Referring to the family as "gentry," and the home as a "manor," the singers say that the head of the household will "live for many years" and have "one thousand sheep and three thousand goats." Wishing good fortune for a home, they sing, "May this house never have a single stone crack."

Because children are considered to be pure and close to God, and because their voices are sweet, the wishes they sing are thought likely to come true. Any house gladly welcomes a performance, and most will invite the children in to sing and have treats. If a family raises chickens, the wife may ask the children for an extra favor. Should the children sit on the floor during their visit, the hens will lay more eggs.

> **Because children are considered to be pure and close to God, and because their voices are sweet, the wishes they sing are thought likely to come true.**

The kálanda are very specific to the people being caroled. At a farmer's home, children sing wishes for healthy animals, fertile soil, and a strong and steady plow. On the islands, they sing to families about seaworthy boats, mild winds, and safe sailing.

Because men on Greek islands mostly have been fishermen or sailors, traditional kálanda lavish praise on the sailing ability of the head of the household:

For you, my lord, an armed frigate would be fit
With towering stern and lion-like prow
To have the mast worked out of brass and rigs made out of wire
To have the sails cut out of silk and sail-yards steely made.

On Crete, the ancient songs even wish luck in the gender of livestock and children:

I bid you good month,
and may you have an all-female herd
And male offspring as your lads.

Lovely as their verses filled with praise and good wishes may be, kálanda singers rarely get to finish a performance. After only the first few verses, the shopkeeper or head of the household will interrupt to offer a reward. People want to give the singers good fortune in return by letting them stop, hurry on, and collect as many rewards as possible. On the island of Limnos, kálanda bands even sing a verse designed to keep things moving:

Go on, my lord, go on and put
Your hand inside your pocket.
Don't spare the gold coins.

In the past, the reward would be fruit, nuts, and sweet pastries. In Kavala, the old custom was for boys to each carry a pointed skewer. Knowing that some families have slaughtered a pig for the Christmas feast, the boys would sing for scraps of cooked meat, going from house to house until every boy had filled his spear to the top with tasty samples. It was also traditional in this region for boys to dress in costumes and makeup and to tie bells to their belts to ring as they went about caroling.

A vendor in Athens sells Christmas triangles called trigona. Beating on triangles is a traditional way to scare away the mischievous Christmas imps called kalikántzari.

On New Year's Eve, which is also the Eve of the Feast of St. Basil, children make decorated boats to honor St. Basil. They carry the boats from house to house as they sing the kálanda. Rewards for kálanda singing are dropped into the boats.

Today, most kálanda singers perform for coins. With their reward in hand and with a final farewell verse ending, "and let us come here next year and for many years to follow," the boys quickly head off to their next stop.

Ancient Roots

The word kálanda comes from the Greek word *kaló*, meaning "to invite or to shout." The roots of the tradition may reach into the distant past. In pagan times, priests wandered from village to village, chanting a kind of kálanda to honor the goddess Cybele, blessing people, performing exorcisms, and collecting money from believers as they went along.

During the Hellenistic period (323 B.C.-146 B.C., the period of Greek history following Alexander the Great's death until Rome took over Greece) prior to Roman rule (146 B.C.-1453), the new year was celebrated during what is now the month of October, in conjunction with the harvest and planting of new crops. Singers hung a branch outside their own doorways that thankful farmers decorated with gifts of wool, nuts, fruit, and little jars of honey and oil.

Kálanda caroling also seems to be connected to the ancient Roman celebration of the new year. Today, Greek children travel from home to home collecting money. In ancient Rome, the Roman citizens paraded before their emperor on the occasion of the new year, giving him money as they passed.

An Enduring Tradition

This oldest of traditions also is the most enduring. Where once only boys traveled from house to house, now they sometimes are joined by girls. In cities, adults also have taken up singing the kálanda, and professional musicians have blended their music with the simple instruments of the children.

Kálanda singers like to keep their traveling group small, making their individual shares of the reward offerings bigger. Typically, there are one or two singers, a couple of triangle players, and maybe a drum to round out the sound.

There may also be violins, guitars, clarinets, harmonicas, lyres, bells, and drums. Kálanda carolers carry with them the triangles, a bag to hold treats or coins collected, and a tapered stick or cane called a *tzoumàka* to knock on house doors. The tzoumàka is different in different regions of Greece. In northern Greece, kálanda bands make fancy canes decorated with geometric shapes and swifts. The canes are said to contain the power of nature that can be given to all things.

The word kálanda comes from the Greek word kaló, meaning "to invite or to shout."

Especially on New Year's Eve, which is also the Eve of the Feast of St. Basil, the children may replace the bag for treats with small decorated boats of paper, tin, or wood. They make the little boats themselves to honor St. Basil. Rewards for kálanda singing are dropped into the boats.

As they sing their songs of good wishes for the coming year, the singers use the canes to tap the family's barn and storehouse to make them full. They tap the walls of the house to make them sturdy, the animals so they will be healthy and multiply, and family members so they will be healthy, successful, and fertile.

Although usually children keep the coins they collect, in some places children sing kálanda to make money to give to orphanages or to the poor, especially on Christmas Eve.

The Coliandra Tradition

One of the most elaborate kálanda traditions takes place in western Macedonia, where the carols are called *coliandra*. Here the children kick off the season of coliandra singing on St. Nicholas Day, December 6. In small groups, boys and girls go around their villages singing:

Bells ring out on Christmas, symbolizing the watch the shepherds kept on the very first Christmas Eve. This monk rings bells at Varlaam Monastery at Meteora Kalambaka.

The Fourth Wise Man

According to a popular Greek version of the story of the Nativity, originally there were four, not three, wise men who set out to follow the star to the Christ child. All four were Persian astronomer-priests, each of a different race, reflecting the diverse population of Persia at the time. These wise men studied and worshiped the stars and their light. Seeing a bright new star, the wise men followed it. The star led them to the Christ child.

On their journey to Bethlehem, the wise men encountered a gravely injured man. One stopped to care for the man and tend to his needs while the three others continued on.

By the time the fourth wise man was able to follow the others, he was too late to see the newborn Christ. Mary, Joseph, and the baby Jesus had fled to Egypt. They went to escape the wrath of King Herod, whose soldiers were killing baby boys to try to rid Israel of this newborn savior. Arriving in Jerusalem, the fourth wise man stayed to rescue other babies there. Though he never reached the star's destination, the fourth wise man is said to have truly found Christ, too, when he ministered to those who were most in need.

Children, the Coliandra are here.
Be prepared, all of you.
Get your sticks
And go to Saint Lias.

Everywhere in western Macedonia, children can be heard on the days leading up to Christmas as they call each other to prepare for the coliandra.

On December 23, children stack wood and hay to build bonfires in town squares or major crossroads in their villages. They dance in a circle around the bonfires, singing the coliandra and playing their triangles, bells, and drums. Often adults join the fun by singing, dancing, and playing fiddles or clarinets. The bonfires and the bells represent the watch the shepherds kept on the very first Christmas Eve.

While the boys are sleeping that night, their mothers place by their beds the things they will need for making their coliandra rounds the next day: the first of many special coliandra cakes they will receive as rewards, a tzoumàka to carry, and a little bag to hold all the treats they will be given.

Starting early the next morning, the boys sing carols at the homes of all the families they know, being sure to include verses praising each member of the house and wishing all good fortune. Like kálanda singers everywhere, they will be rewarded for the good fortune they bring. Here, the offering is coliandra cakes, figs, nuts, sweets, and in the cities, coins.

Street musicians perform the kálanda in Athens. Where once only boys traveled from house to house singing carols, today, in Greek cities, adults also have taken up singing the kálanda, and professional musicians have blended their music with the simple instruments of the children.

The House of God

The outside of a Greek Orthodox church may be lovely, but it is a plain shell compared to the fantastic beauty inside. Christians accustomed to simple religious surroundings may be greatly surprised by the richness of the decoration and design inside a Greek Orthodox church.

The Greek Orthodox religion celebrates the beauty of the material world as God's creation. It recognizes beauty as an essential part of human life and as a great gift from God. In the church, humans shape that beauty to God's glory, offering it back to God in praise and thanksgiving.

A Byzantine church on Aegina Island (below) has a simple but beautiful exterior. The Pantocrator reigns from the dome above Kaisariani Monastery, Athens (right).

Worship in a Greek Orthodox church is a total experience, purposefully engaging people's thoughts, emotions, and senses. Inside a church, people are surrounded by great beauty. The sight of richly colorful and mysterious icons, the entrancing sound of music, the strong scent of incense—all of these are essential parts of the religious experience. All are designed to transport people to the presence of God, to lift them from their everyday existence to experience the truth of God at the deepest level of the soul.

While Orthodox church services are solemn and can be quite long, they express a feeling of joy. Services are always sung or chanted. Orthodoxy states that God dwells within the church.

As one old saying explains, "Let the Christian consider well when he enters the church that he is entering another heaven. That same majesty of God which is in heaven is also in his church, and on this account, the Christian must enter with reverence and awe."

These feelings come naturally when people look upon the icons and illustrations on the walls, high on the ceiling and dome, and on the *iconostasis*, or screen of icons.

Most Orthodox churches are built in the form of a cross. All are divided into three parts: the narthex, or entrance area; the nave, or large central area where the parishioners attend church; and the sanctu-ary, or most sacred part of the church, which contains the Holy Altar.

The iconostasis separates the sanctuary from the nave. On the right-hand side of the iconostasis are the icons of Christ and St. John the Baptist. On the left side are icons of the *Theotokos* (Mother of our Lord) and the individual church's patron saint. The iconostasis symbolizes people being separated from God through sin. The Divine Liturgy brings them close to God again.

An Orthodox church is often small, emphasizing a sense of community among those who worship together there. Some religious services take place in the nave, in the middle of the congregation, reminding everyone that they are an important part of the whole church.

On the dome or ceiling of the church is an icon of Christ the Almighty, the Pantocrator, reigning over heaven and earth. As people look up, all things seem directed toward this image. This vision expresses the essential idea of the religion.

Twelve Days of Merriment and Mischief

At last the long Christmas Lent has ended and Christmas has arrived. The time for fasting and somber reflection is past. Christ is born and the time for celebration is here. The *Dodecameron* has begun: 12 days of merriment and mischief spent in the company of family and friends.

hristmas Day celebration begins early in the morning at church. Some people keep a vigil as they await the coming of Christ. There are church services on Christmas Eve continuing all through the night. Others hear the bells and head to church as early as 5 or 6 a.m. to take part in three or four hours of prayerful reflection, Communion, and the Christmas Day Liturgy.

Christmas Dinner

The long-anticipated Christmas dinner that breaks the lenten fast is a rich and bountiful delight. Most commonly, the meat is turkey. But for some, the tradition is roast pork from a pig slaughtered the day before. Depending on the region, it may also be chicken or even rabbit. In some regions, the custom is to eat chicken for Christmas dinner and pork the following day. The rule is plenty: plenty of dishes and plenty of each!

The meal is for the immediate family only. Christmas Day is not a time of visiting and partying in Greece. It is strictly a family holiday time to stay in your own home with your own relatives. This seems fitting in a country where it is often said that the primary unit of society is the family, not the individual. The Greek family is a tight, deeply connected group whose feelings and thoughts are fully shared. On such a meaningful religious holiday, the family moves through the day as one unit.

The overall mood of Christmas is joyful but somewhat solemn. Around the dinner table, parents talk to children about the story of Christ's birth and what Christ means for the world.

Cutting the Christopsomo

The centerpiece of the meal and the main focus of Christmas celebration in Greece is the *Christopsomo*, or "Christ bread." This is a large, sweet, shaped loaf of bread. It may contain pine nuts, walnuts or almonds, raisins, and bits of dried apricot or other fruits.

This traditional bread is very much like the *Vasilopita*, or Basil's Bread, which will be the centerpiece of the New Year's celebration in another week. The two celebrations are similar because until the 300's, they were one. Both the birth of Christ and the beginning of a new year were celebrated on December 25.

An American-style Santa flies in front of the Vouli (Parliament) Building in Athens.

The centerpiece of the meal and the main focus of Christmas celebration in Greece is the Christopsomo. The head of the household traditionally breaks the fast and ceremoniously cuts the Christopsomo.

When New Year's Day was moved to January 1, the traditions borrowed from New Year's Day were continued on Christmas Day as well.

Traditionally, the Christopsomo is decorated to reflect the profession of the head of the household. A farmer's bread might be decorated with dough shaped into a plow and oxen. A shepherd's loaf is decorated with designs of lambs, goats, or a herd of sheep. A fisherman's bread, a shopkeeper's bread, or a doctor's bread each have their own special designs. Sometimes, little additional loaves are also baked in the shapes of cattle, hens, or sheep. Any extra loaves made to represent the family's livestock are broken up later and fed to the animals to assure their good health in the coming year.

As the first act of breaking the Christmas Lent fast, the head of the household ceremoniously cuts the Christopsomo. First, he makes the sign of the cross over the bread with a knife while saying, "In the name of the Father, the Son, and the Holy Spirit," the holy trinity in Christianity which refers to the unity of God the Father, his Son, Jesus Christ, and the Spirit of Christ who rose from the dead and ascended into heaven. Then he cuts slices, offering them to people in a set order: the first slice is always saved for Christ, then there is one for the poor, one for each member of the family, and one for the house. Each family strictly follows its own tradition about the number of slices and the order in which they are given out.

For some Greek families, it is customary for the father to place a napkin on his head, then break the Christopsomo over his own head, while saying, "In the name of the Father, the Son, and the Holy Spirit." This is because, according to Greek tradition, all wisdom and all goodness come from the head.

In some places, this dinner is called the "Feast of the Holy Virgin." Preparing the Christmas table, the woman of the house first places the Christopsomo in its position of honor in the center. Then she surrounds the loaf with dried figs and other fruits, walnuts, almonds, hazelnuts, apples, and other little delicacies. She also places a pot of honey on the table.

After the Christopsomo has been cut and offered to all, each person also takes a little honey, symbolizing sweetness in life. Before they sit down to the feast, some families then lift the table slightly three times in honor of the Holy Trinity.

Greek cooks are famous around the world for their desserts, including delicious cakes, pastries, and cookies. The traditional

A zaharoplastio, or sweet shop, displays traditional Christmas sweets.

35

treats of the Christmas season show why. After the sweet and fragrant Christopsomo is shared with family to break the Christmas Lent fast, every table is laden with an array of little delights to tempt children and adults alike.

Now every *zaharoplastio*, or sweet shop, is brimming with mountains of sweet delights. In homes all over Greece, cooks are turning out favorites. Sure to be piled high in every shop window and offered in every home at this season are the two traditional Greek Christmas cookies: white, powdery butter cookies called *kourabiéthes*, and oblong, honey-dipped cookies covered with chopped nuts called *melomakárona*. There are also *koulourakia*, or crisp, sweet cookies shaped by hand and covered with sesame seeds, and *loukoumáthes*, which are deep-fried honey balls topped with honey, and of course, *baklavá*, layers of *phíllo* pastry with chopped nuts and honey-flavored syrup.

Christmas Decorations

Greek cities, like cities around the world, light the dark winter night throughout the Christmas season. There are Christmas-light displays in Athens and other cities. Little villages string lights around squares and across streets. Still there is no public celebration before Christmas Day.

One unique Greek twist on holiday decoration is the decorating of boats. Because St. Basil sails from his home in Caesarea to bring presents on New Year's Eve, boats are trimmed with lights and decorations to welcome his arrival. Children also decorate little paper, tin, or wooden boats as decorations within their homes.

The Christmas tree, though it doesn't have deep roots in Greek Christmas tradition, has found a place in many Greek homes during the holiday season. In 1839, a Christmas tree first appeared in Greece in the court of King Othon I, ruler of a newly liberated Greece from the Ottoman Empire. The well-to-do in the king's society quickly followed suit, but the custom spread very slowly through cities and villages elsewhere in Greece. Perhaps this is because Greece's native scrub pine does not lend itself as readily to the custom as do the towering spruces of northern European countries.

In the past, Greek families in some coastal villages used a juniper tree for a Christmas tree. Ornaments were fashioned from walnuts, almonds, and dried figs wrapped in tin foil and tied to the branches with string. Tiny candles were fixed to the

In Greece, a lighted tree stands as a beautiful symbol that everything in nature offers its best to welcome the newborn Christ child. The lights and tinsel also cheer and brighten the dark night, helping to drive away the evil kalikántzari.

How the Pine Tree Became a Christmas Symbol

In the Greek telling of the Nativity story, all the world welcomed the Christ child. Everything in nature offered something to Mary and her newborn baby. In Greece and the world of the Mediterranean, the place where Mary and Joseph found shelter is thought to have been a cave. The cave, representing the earth itself, gave its protection to the family. The angels sang glad tidings of His birth. The shepherds and their flocks came to bow down and give Him praise.

The wise men came bearing fine gifts. The animals in the shelter gave the warmth of their breath and their bodies to keep the baby comfortable. The stars offered their light.

There were three trees growing nearby—a date palm, an olive tree, and a scrub pine. The date palm presented dates for Mary to eat so she would have strength to feed her baby. The olive tree gave oil to use as a salve for healing and soothing.

The poor scrub pine, however, was a plain, lowly tree with nothing useful to offer. Taking pity on the pine, stars came down from the sky and lit on its branches, making the tree a truly wondrous sight to delight the newborn baby.

branches to be lighted only on Christmas Eve and Christmas Day. Today, Greece has its share of Christmas tree farms, and this holiday tradition has taken hold.

In the Greek home, the star atop the tree and its glowing candles or lights represent the light that Christ brought into a dark world. In Greece, a lighted tree also stands as a beautiful symbol of the Greek notion that everything in nature offers its best to welcome the newborn Christ child. The little lights and tinsel also cheer and brighten the dark night, helping to drive away the evil *kalikántzari*, or tricksters who come from deep inside the earth to make mischief at Christmastime.

Following Greek custom, the Christmas tree does not appear until Christmas Eve at the earliest. The time the tree appears varies from home to home. Some decorate the tree for Christmas Day so that it can stand as a beautiful symbol of the light and love Christ brought to the world. In other places, the tree is put up on New Year's Eve in anticipation of the arrival of St. Basil, who comes down the chimney like St. Nicholas does in other countries, and leaves presents for children. The tree may even be left that night for St. Basil himself to decorate.

> **Following Greek custom, the Christmas tree does not appear until Christmas Eve at the earliest.**

Though there may be a tree, Christmas morning does not find presents under it. Christmas Day here is not the time for exchanging presents. Instead, Greek families are likely to celebrate Christ's birth by giving presents to hospitals and orphanages.

In some places in northeastern Greece, a small Greek version of a Christmas tree is an old holiday custom. Families stand an olive branch in the middle of the *Christopsomo*. The olive branch, symbolizing health, is decorated with apples, oranges, nuts, and other little treats.

The Dodecameron

With the break of the Christmas Lent fast, the Dodecameron begins. The Dodecameron, or the 12 days, is the joyful, playful period running from Christmas Day through New Year's Day and ending on Epiphany (January 6). This is a time of great merrymaking, parties, and lighthearted play. The fast is broken, the Christ child has come, and it is time for family, friends, and food.

The Christmas tree, though it doesn't have deep roots in Greek Christmas tradition, has found a place in many Greek homes during the holiday season.

It is also a time when light has great meaning. Following pre-Christian custom, the 12 days are also a symbolic time of moving from the dark days to a return of the light. Both ancient and Christian symbols make this a time of hope, a time when good triumphs over evil and the future looks bright.

In some parts of Greece, devoutly religious women stay awake all night on Christmas Eve, holding a vigil in the belief that, if their faith is strong, they will "see the heavens open" at the moment of Christ's birth. In addition, a light seen in the east that night means a dearly held wish will be granted.

December 25, the day chosen to celebrate Christ's birth, occurs very near the winter solstice, which is when the days begin to grow longer and brighter again. Before Christ was born, December 25 was celebrated as the birthday of Mithras, the Persian god of the sun and victor over darkness.

The 12 days are also a symbolic time of moving from the dark days to a return of the light.

It is fitting that the image of light at Christmas is strong in Greek Orthodox teachings. *"I Yennisi Sou Christe"* (Your Birth, O Christ), a most familiar and beloved Greek Christmas carol, refers to Christ as the "light of knowledge," the "sun of righteousness," and the "dawn from Heaven."

Preparing, Partying

Now Greeks find themselves caught up in the holiday rush that people in other countries experience before Christmas. In the one week between Christmas and New Year's Day, there is decorating and cooking to do and presents to buy and wrap.

Now is the time to celebrate with friends. The Greek word *paréa* means both companionship and a group of friends. And no one in Greece would be without paréa during the holiday season. Friends get together over coffee, again over lunch, for coffee after, for an afternoon drink, and late in the evening for dancing or talk. Together, the paréa now moves through a joyful cycle of Christmas celebration.

With the fast broken, there are dances and parties nearly every night, many delicious foods to eat, and festive places to go. In the city, friends meet at cafés to talk during the day while sampling Christmas treats, then head to holiday dances and parties that last long into the night.

If there is to be a tree or other holiday decoration, this is the time to trim it. Everything needs to be ready for New Year's

Eve parties, St. Basil's arrival, and New Year's Day festivities, all coming in one week.

This is also a great time to be silly. The week between New Year's Day and Epiphany in northern Greece is the time for merrymaking. Following the old "mummers" tradition, people go about dressed in costume. At this time, they may meet pretend animals of all kinds, grannies, rag men, brides and grooms, and more, all out for a night's fun of visiting and partying.

When the Christmas fast is broken, it is time for partying and paréa—companionship with friends.

Kalikántzari: Christmastime tricksters

Kindness and good will abound during the Dodecameron. Joyful gatherings of family and friends follow one after the other. Still, this is no time to let down your guard. Some very determined creatures are about, doing their best to disrupt all this harmony.

Deep within the earth live the kalikántzari, nasty beings who are only happy when they're being really naughty. All year long, the kalikántzari are hard at work underground, chopping or gnawing away at the trunk of the tree of life, a huge tree which is the foundation supporting the earth. Eager

A peaceful chapel
made of rocks stands
by the sea.

to destroy God's work, they are making real progress hacking
the tree trunk. In fact, they have nearly succeeded.

Suddenly, something causes the kalikántzari to stop work
and head for the surface. The story of who they are and why
they stop chopping has changed over the centuries. According
to ancient folklore, the kalikántzari come up because they have
been scared away from their work by *Helios*, the god of the sun.
These little evil beings represent the forces of darkness in the

struggle between good and evil, or darkness and light, which is common to the folklore of many cultures at the time of the winter solstice.

The story of the kalikántzari also may have roots in the beliefs of the ancient Greeks. In the Athens of long ago, it was believed that on one special day each year, the spirits of the dead, discover the gates of Hades ajar and head for the surface to pester the living. Today, on some Greek islands, the kalikántzari still are thought of as spirits of the dead.

With the birth of Christ, this pagan idea, like many others, took on new meaning. Some say the kalikántzari become distracted from their evil work by the joyful sounds of people celebrating the birth of Jesus on Christmas Day. They come aboveground to disrupt this happy noise. Others say that the birth of Jesus caused the tree trunk they were chopping to become whole again, making the nasty creatures furious and sending them stomping to the surface to cause trouble.

Whatever the reason, up the kalikántzari come on Christmas Day. Some say the kalikántzari are little imps or sprites; others insist they are big goblins or trolls. They have been described as huge, ugly, black monsters; as hairy beings with red eyes and hoofs; as short with bow legs; as having horns, pointed ears, claws, cloven hoofs, or a tail. Sometimes they may hold a small trident. No one has ever seen the kalikántzari because they make their mischief under cover of the night.

What has been witnessed is the trouble these creatures cause. During the Dodecameron, the kalikántzari are blamed for spilled milk, lost keys, broken glass, burned dinners, and all kinds of fairly harmless but annoying mishaps.

No prank is too big or too small for these tricksters. Kalikántzari could make all your farm animals sick, put a toad in your shoe, or braid your horse's tail. They can make you put too much salt in the soup, spoil all your food, or cause the fire to go out. They're even said to ride on people's backs just for fun.

Finally, Epiphany comes and the fear of a dousing with holy water forces the kalikántzari to retreat back underground. There, some say, they will stay, chopping away, until Christmas once again disrupts their nasty work.

Kalikántzari represent the forces of darkness in the struggle between good and evil

Keeping
Kalikántzari Away

How do you keep those pesky imps called kalikántzari from wreaking havoc in your home during the holiday season? Fire, light, and holy water offer basic protection. In some small villages, large bonfires are kept burning each night during the holiday period to ward off kalikántzari, and people are careful to carry a lighted candle when they are out after dark. Most safeguards, however, focus on the home.

Because kalikántzari can enter a house through the chimney, some Greek families keep a fire burning in the hearth day and night all through the 12-day period from Christmas to Epiphany. The *skarkántzalos*, or "Christ log," like the English Yule log, serves a twofold purpose. It both warms the home and drives away evil all through the 12-day period.

In the past, a visitor to a Greek home between Christmas and Epiphany would be whisked inside and the door shut right away. Taken straight to the hearth, the visitor would be asked to pick up the poker and prod the fire to make it burn brighter. This maneuver would frighten off any spirits that might have sneaked in behind the visitor. All these rituals would take place right away, even before any greetings were spoken. The kalikántzari must be kept at bay.

Fortunately, the kalikántzari are simpleminded, so one little trick works wonders. Place a sieve over the chimney flue or a colander behind the door. The troublemakers will stop in their tracks and feel compelled to count all the holes. They'll be kept busy for hours, stopping for long stretches every time they need to say "three," the symbol for the Holy Trinity, as they count. Before the kalikántzari can finish, it will be dawn and time for them to flee.

Some traditional kalikántzari preventions are designed to repel them. Burn an old, smelly shoe or some foul-smelling plants, or throw salt into the fire and make a frightening noise. Nail the lower jaw of a pig up behind the door.

Other preventions work by soothing their nasty spirits. In Aghialo, people mix up a treat of wheat, raisins, walnuts, and figs and throw it up the chimney for the kalikántzari to enjoy. In Cyprus, the kalikántzari snack is thrown onto the roof.

In some places, the tradition is to throw pancakes onto the roof on the night before *Theophania* (Epiphany), so that when the tricksters finally go away for this year, they go with a final good thought about the people in that house. Some people hang a sausage on a hook by the fireplace as a parting gift to the kalikántzari. In northern Greece, holy water is only part of the kalikántzari solution. On the Eve of Theophania, young men travel around dressed in wild and frightening costumes and jingling bells to scare the little imps off.

Some say the *kálanda* that children sing from house to house on special nights dur-

ing the Christmas season originally were intended to frighten away the kalikántzari of the season. For this purpose, the wilder the singing and the noisier the instruments, the better. By ringing triangles, beating drums, and singing with all their might, children present a powerful force for good.

Since kalikántzari are creatures of the night and the dark, the bright lights of a city, especially when everything shines with twinkling Christmas decorations, can keep the little devils away. In the home, a Christmas tree aglow with lights and shiny ornaments is a strong repellent, too.

Kalikántzari prevention also is behind the most common household symbol of the Christmas season. In nearly every home, you will find a sprig of basil hanging from a string suspended over a shallow wooden bowl of water. From time to time, family members dip the basil in the water, then use it to shake protective drops around the rooms of the house to keep them all free of kalikántzari.

On the evening of the Epiphany, the last night of the Dodecameron, the kalikántzari leave. Some say they go back to their tree chopping until next Christmas, when they come back to bother mortals again. Others think kalikántzari become like mortals themselves after the Epiphany. Like teasing dancers, these once evil spirits become our friends, which is the final message of reconciliation of the Dodecameron.

In some small villages, large bonfires are kept burning each night during the holiday period to ward off kalikántzari. The bonfire also recalls the vigil the shepherds kept when Christ was born.

Ending One Year, Beginning Another

From start to finish, New Year's Eve and New Year's Day in Greece provide an opportunity to see into the future and perhaps even influence the future. Nearly everything people do on these two special days has the power to predict or determine their luck in the year to come.

New Year's Eve Day is off to a fortunate start when children tap on your door to ask if they may sing the *kálanda*. Tomorrow is St. Basil's Day, and they are anticipating St. Basil's arrival and wishing you well. The songs they sing bring good wishes and good fortune for the year ahead.

Housewives hurry the singers inside because having a kálanda singer in the house is lucky. It's even better if they sit on the floor. It means your chickens will sit, too, and lay more eggs. In some regions, the kálanda singers even act like chickens, clucking and running wildly from house to house.

The singers may carry an apple or an orange, symbols of plenty; a little ship in honor of St. Basil, or a paper star; plus a stick. A tap from a kálanda singer's stick can bring a bright future to a person or an animal, to a house, a shop, a boat, or a farmer's field.

A Night of Fun and Anticipation

Throughout New Year's Eve Day, there is cooking and busy preparation for the night and the excitement to come. Everyone will stay up tonight. Some women will cook for the feast to come, others will keep a vigil to see the new year in safely, but most will celebrate seeing the new year in with family and friends.

New Year's Eve is the best night for a party. This is the night for card games. Card games and other games of chance and skill will continue for hours in homes, at parties, and at local cafés and restaurants. Cards may begin after a lavish dinner or be played while enjoying coffee and sweets such as *loukoumáthes*. The games are friendly and fun, but everyone dearly wants to win. When all the cards or bets are counted this night, the winner will be the lucky one in the year ahead and the loser will be the not-so-lucky one.

Looking for a Lucky Year

If chicken is part of their New Year's Eve dinner, a family will have another chance to see into the future. After the meal, the oldest person in the house examines the chicken's breastbone. If it is dark in color, the family will thrive and prosper. If the breastbone is pale and transparent, poverty will visit the house.

Athens rings in a New Year with fireworks over the ancient Acropolis.

At midnight on New Year's Eve, many families throw open all the windows of their houses, sending out all the evil spirits and bad luck of the previous year. Some families turn all the lights out as midnight nears. They switch them back on at midnight. As the new year arrives, happy shouts of *"Kalí Chroniá!"* (Good year) and *"Chrónia pollá!"* (Many years) are heard everywhere.

Welcoming St. Basil

This night, Greek children are not thinking about the year to come. Their hopes are pinned on tomorrow morning. New Year's Day is also the Feast Day of St. Basil. Tonight, while children are sleeping, St. Basil will come by boat from his home in Caesarea, bringing presents for all the children. No one sees St. Basil. He comes and goes silently in the night. Still, every family is sure to prepare a fine welcome for him and make him a part of the family's New Year's Day celebration.

In Lesbos, it is the custom to stand a long log upright in the fireplace so St. Basil can step down without effort. On the island of Skyros, people prepare a special tray for him. It holds a bowl of water, two dishes of pancakes or other sweet cakes, a pomegranate, and a pestle or stone. When you help St. Basil refresh

Greeks decorate model ships for Christmas and in honor of St. Basil.

himself and sweeten his tongue, he will help keep your house "fresh and sweet" all year long.

A child might also place a little purse with a few coins in it for St. Basil to bless when he arrives. In the morning, the child will find the coins in the purse have been blessed—and have multiplied.

The First to Arrive

Before midnight arrives on New Year's Eve, each household selects the right person to step across the threshold first in the new year. This is the person who can bring good fortune to the entire house in the coming year. Who's the right person?

In some regions, the first through the door must be the head of the household, the oldest son, or the youngest child. Elsewhere, people choose a "lucky" child, defined as any person with two living parents.

The actual first to arrive may be an icon, because it is traditional for the first person to arrive to hold an icon in front of him or her, letting it cross the threshold first. When the first visitor steps in, people say "kaló potharikó," in the wish that this person will bring good luck.

> Genuine happiness on the part of the newly arrived person will mean real happiness for the home this year.

Some families don't send someone special out to come in first, but leave the first arrival of the new year to chance. They hope their first visitor will be someone strong and healthy. Should such a person cross the threshold first, he or she will be greeted with sweet pastries or coins.

The temperament of the first to arrive is significant, too. Should someone arrive who is naturally grumpy or morose, the family members will quickly offer the person sweets and do all they can to make him or her feel truly happy. Genuine happiness on the part of the newly arrived person will mean real happiness for the home this year.

Sometimes the first in is not a person at all. In the village of Kavala, a family would take a sheep or a goat to the door of the house and watch how it stepped in. If the animal entered on its right foot first, that signaled fortune and happiness in the coming year.

The first-in ritual can be quite complicated in some places in Greece. On the island of Amorgos, a member of the family is assigned the job. This person must enter the house coming from church and holding a small icon. Taking two steps into the house, the person says, "Come in good luck." Taking two steps back out, he or she says, "Out, ill luck." The in-and-out procedure is repeated two more times.

Coming in for the third time, the selected first-to-arrive throws a pomegranate down, causing it to split open and reveal its rich bounty of seeds, symbolic of abundance in the year to come.

Next everyone present dips a finger in honey and has a taste, hoping that the coming year will be this sweet. Finally the family eats a sample of boiled wheat and praises St. Basil, hoping for health and prosperity in the year ahead.

In Crete, the first to enter a house in the new year should be a stranger. And the person should behave rather strangely. Bringing in a large stone, he or she places it in the middle of the room and sits down on it. From this lowly perch, the person recites:

"Good day to you, happy new month. Blessings upon your poultry, your lambs, and your goats. May your hen sit on her eggs. May your cow give birth to a calf. May your she-ass give birth to a mule. Female lambs and kids to you and male children. And may gold the weight of this stone enter your house."

Like the kálanda singers, this stranger will be rewarded for his or her kind words with pastries and sweets.

A Very Holy Day

New Year's Day begins with a morning church service. In addition to being the start of a new year and the Feast Day of St. Basil, this holy day is also the day on which the circumcision of Christ is remembered. According to Orthodox tradition, it was at the moment of his circumcision that Christ was named Jesus, the name given to him by an angel.

Cutting the Vasilopita

The most important customary food for New Year's Eve and New Year's Day—maybe even for the entire holiday season—is the *Vasilopita*, or "Basil's Bread," presented in honor of St. Basil. In some regions, this is a cake; in others, a sweet bread. This special bread is round and surrounded with nuts, dried fruits, and sweets. The Vasilopita is baked with a single coin hidden inside. Everywhere, the tradition and the meaning behind the Vasilopita is the same.

The Vasilopita, or "Basil's Bread," is presented in honor of St. Basil on New Year's Day. Good luck will come to the person who gets the slice with the coin baked inside.

The most meaningful moment of New Year's Day and St. Basil's Day comes when the head of the household ceremoniously cuts the Vasilopita. This may occur at the stroke of midnight on New Year's Eve, in the morning of New Year's Day, or at the start of the dinner on New Year's Day.

In many families, the ceremony begins with the singing of a new year's kálanda, or *"kálanda protochrónias"*:

It's the start of the month
and the start of the year,
Oh, my tall rosemary tree,
and the start of a happy new year,
Oh, my church of the holy throne.

St. Basil is coming,
as you noblemen know,
from Caesarea.
You, my lady, are a noblewoman.

The family ceremony also may open with this traditional poem recited by a child:

I take the knife and put it
in my father's hand,
So he can cut the Vasilopita
and give one slice to me.

Then, the head of the household takes the knife and makes the sign of the cross over the bread, saying, "In the name of the Father, the Son, and the Holy Spirit, Amen."

The bread is cut, and pieces are handed out carefully in a special order. The first piece is for Christ, and will be placed in the family's *ikonostási*, or family altar. There will be pieces for the Virgin Mary, for St. Basil, and a piece for the needy. Then, pieces will be cut for members of the family, again in order. First, the head of the household, then each member in order, including those who are absent, plus a piece for the house and one for the farm. On the islands, there may be a piece cut for the family's boat.

The number of pieces cut, and the exact order, varies from house to house, but always begins with Christ and/or St. Basil, and there will always be a piece for the less fortunate. If the Vasilopita is cut at midnight, the piece for St. Basil will be left out for him to find on his visit that night.

Greek fishermen repair fishing nets on the Island of Ios in the Cyclades. Because men on Greek islands mostly have been fishermen or sailors, traditional kálanda lavish praise on the sailing ability of the head of the household.

Handing out the pieces, the father or other head of the household wishes each person in turn "Chrónia pollá" or "Kalí chroniá." One person will have a wonderful start to the year, for one piece will contain the hidden coin. Finding the coin in your piece brings luck for the entire year to come.

How did the tradition of the Vasilopita begin?

The ancient Greeks had a custom of baking breads at the start of a new year to present to their gods and to offer to their friends as symbols of good luck in the coming year. This may be the very distant beginnings of the current tradition.

The custom of a hidden coin and of pieces designated for St. Basil, for the house, and for the poor go back to St. Basil's generosity. Exactly how it all began is the subject of legends. Every family knows a story demonstrating St. Basil's intelligence and kindness.

One legend says that St. Basil held all the gold, silver, and jewelry of the people of Caesarea in safekeeping. Why? Maybe he had recovered the riches from thieves or had collected them all for a tax that was then canceled.

When he wanted to return the valuables, the people disagreed about who should get what. St. Basil told them to bake all the items into a cake. When the cake was cut, each piece miraculously held exactly what that person should receive.

A rich spread on this day symbolizes prosperity and plenty for the year ahead.

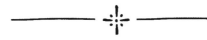

A Good Year Ahead

Plenty of time will be devoted on New Year's Eve and New Year's Day to preparation of the New Year's Day and St. Basil's Day feast. This meal is the most lavish and sumptuous of all the feast day dinners, for a rich spread on this day symbolizes prosperity and plenty for the year ahead.

Pomegranates, sweets, and honey—all symbols of abundance—may be placed on the table. There may also be an olive branch representing health or coins for prosperity.

While Christmas dinner is strictly a family meal, New Year's Day is the time to throw open the door and welcome extended family, neighbors, and friends. The meal resembles the Christmas feast, but on a grander scale. There will likely be roast pork, or chicken or turkey, plus a wide assortment of vegetable dishes, breads, and pastries.

A place at the table will be set for St. Basil. In some parts of Greece, the tradition is to leave a rich table full of food out all night, so St. Basil can enjoy the feast whenever he arrives. Other families set a place for the poor and leave the windows and doors open wide to welcome any passing stranger to come and share their meal, following St. Basil's example of generosity and kindness.

Good Fortune and Happiness

The wonderful New Year's Day feast is not the only symbol of good to come in the year ahead. In fact, it is generally believed that "As goes New Year's Day, so goes the new year."

There is plenty people can do personally to influence their own year ahead. They can try to be the first to see something good or hear happy news. They can make the first thing they eat on New Year's Day something sweet to make the whole year sweet. They can wear something new to brighten the year ahead.

Other new year's traditions bring fortune to the house itself and everyone within.

Most important, they can try to be happy and kind all day. They don't argue, cry, or act mean. They are careful not to lose anything. Whatever they do this day, they will do all year.

Other new year's traditions bring fortune to the house itself and everyone within. Some people break a pomegranate over the threshold, insuring plenty. In many places, it is customary to kill a rooster on the threshold, thereby making the house strong and sturdy. From this rooster, the traditional avgolémeno soup of New Year's Day is made.

Some people bring a stone or sand into the house on New Year's Day. The heavier the stone or the more grains of sand, the fuller the harvest in the year ahead.

In Arachova, people leave a stone and a pomegranate out under the stars on New Year's Eve. In the morning, a family member throws both the stone and the pomegranate into the house, saying, "Strong as a stone, full as a pomegranate."

The weather on New Year's Day is significant. If it's fair, the weather will remain good for at least 40 days. Shepherds even observe the position of sleeping sheepdogs on this day. Dogs lying in the right position provide another good omen.

One complicated ritual blends Christian ideas into an ancient pagan custom for renewing the health and prosperity of a house.

On New Year's Day, every jug and pitcher in the house must be emptied and refilled with fresh "Basil's" water.

Heading to the well to refill their jugs, women on the island of Skyros carry along figs, currants, and nuts. They will throw these little treats into the well as offerings to the *Nereid*, a sea nymph who lives there.

In some places, the trip to the well and back must be made by a child who utters not a single word on the journey coming and going. At the well, he or she throws corn in the water, saying, "May riches flow as water flows." Returning home in silence, the child gives the water to the family. Everyone then must drink and wash with the new water.

In another variation on this tradition, young women walk silently to the well, carrying sweets with them. At the well, they leave their sweets and pick up any left by others. They also scoop up a handful of sand. When they return home, they throw the sand on the floor. The number of grains of sand tell

Breaking a pomegranate on New Year's Day ensures plenty.

55

The first person to step through the doorway on New Year's Day may bring good luck to a Greek household. This woman stands in her doorway in the island of Naxos.

how much fortune and happiness the family will have in the year ahead.

Open Doors, Open Hearts

On New Year's Day, presents are exchanged between family members and friends. Godparents make a point of visiting every godchild they have and giving each a special present. This quickly leads to a party in every house. The fun that begins on this day will continue for days. Fasting is called off and everyone can eat all good things. Parties continue until the fast day that begins Epiphany.

St. Basil

St. Basil the Great, one of the most revered saints in the Greek Orthodox religion, is the most anticipated visitor of the Christmas season—next to the Christ child. He doesn't put in a personal appearance on a sleigh or riding a donkey, but he comes and goes unseen on New Year's Eve, leaving evidence of his generosity and kindness to children behind. Although St. Basil shares the title of patron saint of children with St. Nicholas, in Greece, St. Basil's generosity on New Year's Day has earned him first place in the hearts of children and adults alike.

St. Basil is considered one of the three great leaders of the church, along with St. Gregory the Theologian and St. John Chrysostom. The three share the title of patron saint of education. During his lifetime in the 300's, St. Basil was both an intellectual driving force behind the formation of the Greek Orthodox religion and a living example of faith and kindness in his everyday dealings with people. St. Basil wrote the church's Divine Liturgy, created the rules for monastic life, became a gifted preacher, and served as bishop of Caesarea, a city in ancient Cappadocia in Asia Minor (now Kayseri, Turkey).

St. Basil was born in Caesarea into a wealthy Christian family and studied both in Constantinople and Athens. During a visit to

> St. Basil is one of Greece's most revered saints. His feast day is on New Year's Day.

Egypt, he was taken by the holiness of the desert hermits he saw and decided to become a monk himself.

Educated in Greek philosophy and science, St. Basil chose to spend his life as a missionary among the common people, working for social reform and justice. Credited with founding the first orphanage, St. Basil is the patron saint of orphans. He also established the first Christian charitable institutions to care for the sick, the poor, and the elderly. Because of his kind works fostering the welfare of others, St. Basil is the patron saint of children, of education, and of the poor.

The New Year's *Vasilopita*, or Basil's bread, is part of the most significant tradition of the entire Christmas holiday season. Legend has it that the Vasilopita first came into being because St. Basil was concerned about the plight of poor families in his village. He looked for a way to help without humiliating them. He went to a local baker with a sack of gold coins. He told the baker to bake many loaves of bread, each with a coin hidden inside. These loaves were distributed to poor families. People were able to get help through this seeming stroke of good fortune.

Today, Greek children wait eagerly each New Year's Eve for St. Basil to sail from his home in Caesarea. When they are sleeping, he will come down the chimney, bringing gifts from the kindness of his heart.

Epiphany

Epiphany, also called *Theophania* (God appears), is the third major holiday of the Greek Orthodox Church during the Christmas holiday period. In religious importance, Epiphany follows only Easter and Christmas. Its arrival signals the end of the *Dodecameron*, the 12-day period of celebration for Christmas and the New Year.

he observance of Theophania is spread across three days: January 5, the Eve of Theophania, also called the Lesser Blessing of the Water; January 6, Theophania, or the Greater Blessing of the Water; and January 7, the feast day of St. John the Baptist.

The blessing of the water, that is the primary religious event of these days, reflects Jesus's baptism in the River Jordan by John the Baptist and God's revelation to the world of Jesus as his son.

A Final Round of Kálanda Singing

The morning of the Eve of Epiphany brings *kálanda* singers to doorsteps once more. This time, the children announce the baptism of Christ. They sing:

Epiphany has come,
illumination of the world,
and great rejoicing in the Lord.

By Jordan River,
stands our good Mary,
and thus she begs St. John:

"St. John Baptist,
it is in your power
to baptize the child of God."

Blessing the Waters

The Eve of Epiphany is again the occasion for a strict fast and prayerful reflection. Worshipers prepare to receive the newly blessed water and to receive Christ by cleansing their bodies and souls. Some fast on the day before the Eve of Epiphany, so that they are prepared to participate in both the Lesser and the Greater Blessing services. Others fast on the Eve of Epiphany and attend the second-day service only. The Lesser and the Greater Blessing services are similar.

During the Lesser Blessing service, the priest calls on the Holy Spirit to sanctify the water. He then dips a cross into the water three times, symbolizing Jesus's baptism in the River Jordan.

On January 6, the Greater Blessing of the Water takes place. In the country-side, on the islands, and along the coast, the blessing takes place alongside a nat-ural body of water.

Then people come forward to be blessed with this holy water. The priest dips a large sprig of basil or a small evergreen branch into the water. As he touches the wet sprig to each worshiper's head, he says, "*Chrónia pollá*," or "Good year."

The parishioner then kisses the cross and the priest's hand and is given a little bottle of the holy water to take home. Water blessed by a priest at Epiphany is said to heal and to spiritually cleanse the faithful. It is a powerful force against evil in the world.

On January 6, the Greater Blessing of the Water takes place. This may be in a church. However, in the countryside, on the islands, and along the coast, the blessing takes place alongside a natural body of water.

Water blessed by a priest at Epiphany is said to heal and to spiritually cleanse the faithful.

Now a grand procession of altar boys, priests, church officials, and local leaders makes its way from the church to the edge of the water. Icons big and small are carried above their heads. Flowers line the route.

The priest blesses the body of water and throws a large cross into it. At that moment, church bells ring. The harbor is filled with decorated boats of all sizes. All of them will blow their whistles, ring their bells, or fire their guns in celebration.

As soon as the cross hits the water, young men from the village dive in to rescue it. The one who retrieves the cross is formally blessed and is said to have earned good luck for the whole year to come.

Blessing the Home

Armed with fresh holy water, families are ready now to drive away the *kalikántzari*, who have been bothering them all through the holidays. A few sprinkles around the house should do the trick.

In Greek villages everywhere, a priest will visit every home to bless it with holy water at the start of this new year. Before the priest, people clean all the rooms thoroughly and make sure every door is open and every room is lighted. A bowl of clean water, a lighted candle, an icon, and an incense burner are put out on a table.

The priest first dips a cross into the water to bless it. Then, using a sprig of basil, he shakes drops of the holy water into the

four corners of every room, ridding the entire house not just of kalikántzari, but of all kinds of evil spirits.

Afterward, the family uses this holy water to further protect their home. Family members drink some holy water or use it to wash their hands. Sprinkling holy water, they bless the barn, their animals, and their fields of crops.

Unused holy water is carefully saved in a bottle in the *ikonostási*, the home altar. The holy water can be used during the year to chase evil spirits from the house, to help heal a sick person, to protect someone going on a trip, to bless a new enterprise, or whenever people feel they need its healing grace.

Feast Day of St. John the Baptist

The Christmas holiday season in Greece closes on a merry note. The feast day of St. John the Baptist, January 7, is an occasion when houses everywhere in Greece welcome friends and family to share in happy celebration.

In the Greek Orthodox religion, St. John, who baptized Jesus in the River Jordan, holds a position of great honor. An icon of St. John is always placed in a position of honor at Jesus's

During the Greater Blessing of the Water, a priest blesses the body of water and throws a large cross into it. As soon as the cross hits the water, young men from the village dive in to rescue it. The one who retrieves the cross is formally blessed and is said to have earned good luck for the whole year to come.

As almost every family has a John who is celebrating his name day, this feast day is especially festive.

St. John, who baptized Jesus in the River Jordan, holds a position of great honor in the Greek Orthodox religion. His feast day is celebrated January 7.

left side on the screen of icons, or *iconostasis*, that separates the nave from the sanctuary in a Greek Orthodox church. Because he baptized Jesus, St. John is the patron saint of godparents.

In Greece, where loving godparents play an essential role in guiding and nurturing the children under their charge, St. John is a much revered and much loved figure. It is no surprise that John, in its Greek forms, *Yianni* and *Yianna*, is a popular name. As almost every family has a John who is celebrating his name day, this feast day is especially festive.

There is an old Greek saying, *"Spíti horís Yiánni prokopí then káni."* It declares simply, "A home without a person named John will not succeed."

January 8: More Merriment

In some areas of Greece, the festive spirit begun during the Dodecameron, continues through January 8. In Volakas, a community in Drama, Macedonia, this is the day of the *arkoudes* (bears). Men dress as bears, wearing goatskin, a mask, and a bell attached to their belt. In their right hand, they hold a foot of a goat, which they use to strike those in their path. The bear "leaders" dress in old clothes and wear makeup smudged on their faces. They carry musical instruments and dance in a circle, as they scare away passersby by ringing a bell.

Next comes "the wedding." A priest performs this mock ceremony dressed in black with a blanket on his back. He uses a sprig of basil dipped in holy water to sprinkle the wedding guests and wedding party. A group goes to fetch the best man, and then the "bride": a man dressed in traditional white veil and gown. A donkey loaded with the bride's dowry in two chests sets out to the village square. A child sits on the donkey to symbolize fertility. At the bride's house, refreshments are served, and guests, wearing their best clothes, sing as if they were at a real wedding.

At first the bride pretends as though "she" does not want to marry the groom. But later she is persuaded and goes to the square where the marriage takes place with customary formalities and crowns of wire. After the ceremony everyone joins in the dancing and singing. Guests pin money on the clothes of the "bride and groom." This money is then given to the church.

In some areas of Greece, January 8 is "the day of the bears." Men dress as bears, wearing goatskin, a mask, and a bell attached to their belt. In their right hand they hold a foot of a goat, which they use to strike those in their path.

A mock wedding is held in Macedonia on January 8, after the procession of the bears. A man dresses as a bride, and after the ceremony there is music and dancing. Guests pin money on the clothes of the "bride and groom." This money is then given to the church.

This day is also a fun reversal of roles for Greek villagers in Monokklisia, Serres. On this day, according to tradition, the roles normally played by men are undertaken by women, while the men stay at home and do all the women's jobs (washing, cooking, cleaning, feeding the children, etc.). At dawn, the women go out in the streets and wake up the whole village with their shouts and with *tsambounes* (a kind of bagpipe) and drums, giving notice to the men that the village is now under the rule of women.

The women occupy the offices of the commune and the public buildings and ring the church bell. Two women make a round with a bronze platter collecting money. They then draw the budget of the day, while others are gathering provisions for the evening feast. Some women sit in coffee shops, drinking and smoking, while others walk through the streets holding rifles. The men, once they are done with their chores, sit quietly drinking coffee and gossiping. Not all are well behaved. If they go out in the streets and the women catch them, they soak them in water or undress them and make a public spectacle of them. The only male allowed out is the priest, who gives his blessing to the proceedings. In the evening, the women wear their best clothes and go to the coffee shop to drink and engage in "men's talk." There is plenty of drinking, dancing, and singing, until the next day when the rule is handed back to the men.

Old-Fashioned Ornaments

In the past, these ornaments were used to decorate the Christmas tree, which was often a juniper tree.

Materials

Whole walnuts, or
    almonds,
Aluminum foil

Thread
Needle
Permanent markers

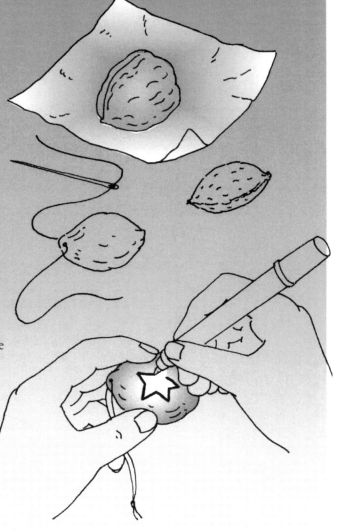

1. Wrap a whole walnut or almond in just enough aluminum foil to cover. Press hard on the foil to allow the details of the nut to show through.

2. Thread a needle with 4 to 6 inches of thread. Bring the needle through the aluminum foil at the top of the ornament so that there is an equal amount of thread on either side of the ornament. Cut the thread and tie the ends together.

3. If you'd like, you can color the ornament using permanent markers. Allow the ink to dry thoroughly.

St. Basil's Bowl

A sprig of basil hanging from a string suspended over a shallow bowl of water is used to protect the home from kalikántzari.

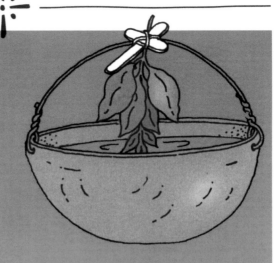

Materials

Brown paint
  (nonwashable)
Paintbrush
Sealer
Sprig of basil
6 in. wire
Small wooden cross (found in craft stores—if you can't find one, glue together two miniature craft sticks in the shape of a cross and allow to dry)

If making a papier-mâché bowl:
2 cups boiling water
1/2 cup all-purpose flour
2 cups cold water
Small plastic bowl
3 T. sugar
Newspaper
Oil
If not making a papier-mâché bowl:
Small, disposable paper or plastic bowl

1. To make a papier-mâché bowl, bring two cups of water to a boil. Mix together the flour and cold water in a bowl. Add this mixture to the boiling water and allow it to return to a boil. Remove from heat and stir in the sugar. As the mixture cools, it will thicken. Let cool to room temperature.

2. Cover your work area with plenty of newspaper. Turn the plastic bowl upside down on your work area. Lightly coat the bottom surface of the bowl with oil. This will allow your papier-mâché bowl to slip off when dry.

3. Tear (don't cut) narrow strips of newspaper. Dip the strips into the paste, coating completely. As you lift the strips out, run them between your thumb and forefinger to squeeze out excess paste. Then drape the strips across the bowl. Overlap strips slightly as you go—the torn edges will blend together and your final bowl will have a smoother finish.

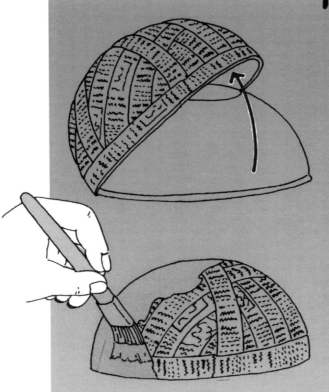

4. Allow the papier-mâché to dry—about a day or two. Then slip your new bowl off of the plastic bowl.

5. When the bowl is completely dry, cover it with sealer and allow to dry. If you are using a disposable paper or plastic bowl, cover it with sealer and allow to dry.

6. Paint the bowl brown. This will make it look more like the traditional wooden bowl. When dry, coat the bowl with another coat of sealer. This will allow you to add a small amount of water to the bowl.

7. Cut a length of wire long enough to stretch across the top of the bowl. Wrap a sprig of basil around the wooden cross, and then wrap the center of the wire around the basil and cross.

8. Poke a hole on either side of the rim of the bowl. Thread one end of the wire through one of the holes, stretch the wire across the bowl, and thread the other end of the wire through the other hole. The cross and basil should hang down in the center of the bowl. Put enough water in the bowl so that the basil touches the water.

Paper Boat

Children make little boats to honor
St. Basil who travels by ship from his
home in Caesarea bringing presents to
Greek children.

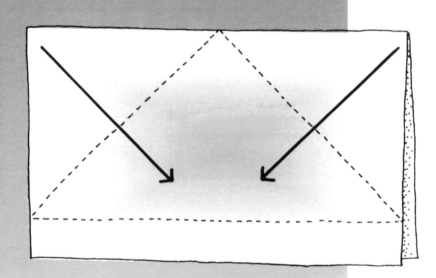

Materials

8 1/2 in. x 11 in.
piece of paper
Stickers
Glitter
Glue
Marker or crayons

1. Fold the piece of paper in half.

2. Fold down the top corners so that
the edges meet in the middle.

3. Fold the bottom edge up, turn the
paper over and turn the other edge
up. Pull open the paper and flatten it
sideways into a diamond shape.

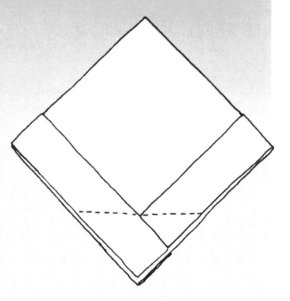

4. Turn the bottom corner up, then turn the paper over and turn the other corner up. Again, open the paper from the bottom and flatten it sideways.

5. Gently pull the ends out, then fold the bottom up. You have a boat!

6. Decorate your boat with the stickers, glitter, glue, markers, and/or crayons.

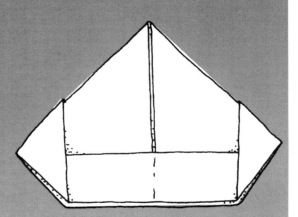

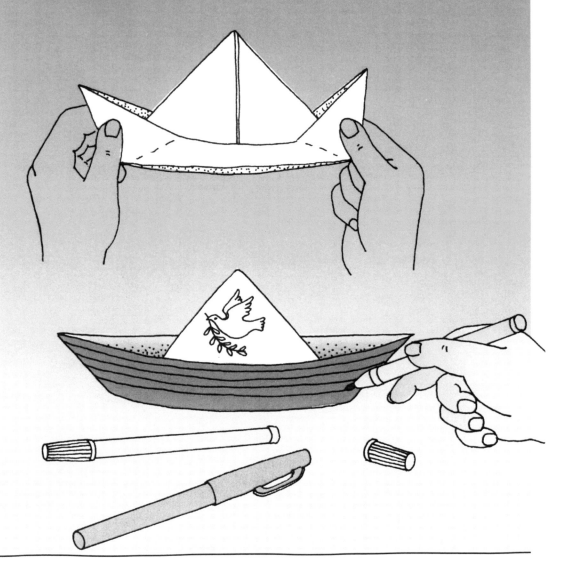

Christmas Candleholder

This festive candleholder will bring a warm glow to your home during the Christmas season. Fire is also another way to keep kalikántzari away!

Materials

Medium-sized glass jar
Paintbrush
Tea light
Glue
Red or green water-based craft paint
Craft knife or scissors
Heavy, dark blue colored paper

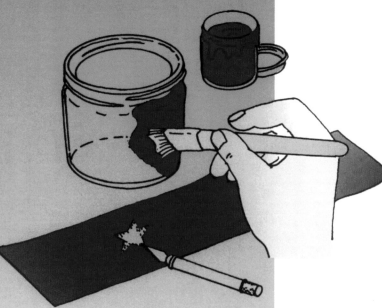

1. Paint the entire outside surface of the jar.

2. Cut the paper to fit around the outside of the jar. Cut Christmas shapes, such as stars or Christmas trees, out of the paper. Have an adult help you with the craft knife.

3. Glue the paper to the outside of the jar.

4. Place the tea light inside the jar.

5. Have an adult light the candle. Watch the colored cutouts glow through the dark paper.

I Yennisi Sou Christe
(Your Birth, O Christ)

I - yén - ni - sí sou Chri - sté o THe ós i

món. a - né - ti - le to kó - smo to fos to tis

gnó - se - os en af - ti gar i tis á - stris la-

trév - on - des i - po a - sté-ros e - thi - thá-skon-do.

Se pro - ski - nin ton í - li - on tis thi - ke - o-

si - nis ke se yi - nó - skin ex i - psous a-

na - to - lín. Ky - ri - e, thó - xa si.

Your birth, O Christ our God, brought to the world the light of knowledge.
For through it those who had adored the stars were taught by a star to worship
you, the sun of righteousness, and to know you as the dawn from heaven,
O Lord, glory to you.

Kálanda Christouyennon
(Christmas Kálanda)

1. Ka - lín es - pé - ra - n ár - chon -
2. ná - te si - me -

tes, ki a - n i - ne
ron stin vi - THle -

o - ri - smós sas, Chri - stoú ti
é - m tin pó - li, i ou - ra -

THí - a yén - ni - si
ni a - gál - lon - te

na i - pó st'ar - chon - ti - kó
ke ke her' - i phí - sis

sas. 2. Chris - tós yen - ó - li.

1. Good evening, noble folk. If you so command,
   I will tell your noble household of the birth of Christ.
2. Today Christ is being born in Bethlehem,
   and the heavens rejoice along with all of nature.

Cucumber-Yogurt Dip

1 medium cucumber
1 clove garlic, finely chopped
3 green onions, finely chopped
1 tsp. olive oil

1/2 tsp. white vinegar
1/2 tsp. dried dill weed
1 container (8 oz.) plain, low-fat
    yogurt

Peel cucumber, cut it in half lengthwise, and scoop out the seeds. Then cut the cucumber into small chunks. In a small bowl, mix cucumber with garlic, green onions, olive oil, vinegar, and dill weed. Add yogurt and stir gently to combine. Cover and chill in the refrigerator for 2 hours. Serve as a dip with pita bread and/or raw vegetables.

Makes 6 servings

Spanakopita (Spinach Pie)

2 lbs. fresh spinach
2 tbsp. olive oil
1/2 cup green onions, finely
    chopped
1/2 lb. feta cheese, crumbled

1/2 lb. cottage cheese
salt and white pepper, to taste
6 eggs, well beaten
1/2 lb. phíllo pastry
1 1/2 cups (3 sticks) butter, melted

Preheat oven to 350 °F. Remove the large, tough stems from the spinach leaves. Then, rinse, chop, and drain the spinach and place it in a large bowl. Set aside. In a large skillet, heat the oil over medium-high heat. Add the green onions and sauté for about 4 minutes, stirring constantly. Add the onions, feta cheese, cottage cheese, and salt and pepper to the spinach. Carefully fold the beaten eggs into the spinach mixture and set aside.

Coat a 9-inch x 13-inch baking pan with cooking spray. Place 1 sheet of phíllo dough in the pan. Brush the sheet with melted butter, then put another sheet on top of it. Continue adding sheets, brushing each one with butter, until there are 7 sheets. Spread spinach mixture evenly over the phíllo. Place 7 more sheets of phíllo over the spinach, again one at a time, brushing each sheet with melted butter before adding the next. Brush the top of the pie with plenty of butter. Refrigerate the pie for about an hour and then score it into squares with the top of a sharp knife. Do not cut all the way through the pie. Bake in a preheated 350 °F oven for 1 hour or until a light golden color. Cool on a wire rack and cut into squares before serving.

Makes 8 servings

Moussaka

1 1/2 lbs. ground round
1 medium onion, chopped
1 tsp. garlic powder
1 tbsp. oregano
salt and pepper to taste
1 can (8 oz.) tomato sauce
1/2 cup water
1/4 cup vegetable oil

3 medium potatoes, peeled and
    sliced into 1/2-inch slices
2 small eggplants
olive oil
5 tbsp. butter or margarine
1/2 cup flour
2 cups milk
1 cup grated fresh parmesan cheese

Preheat oven to 350 °F.

In a large frying pan or electric skillet, brown ground round and onion. Drain fat. Add spices, tomato sauce, and water. Simmer 10 minutes. Remove from pan and set aside. Wipe pan with a paper towel. Add oil to pan and heat over medium-high heat. Add potatoes and brown quickly on both sides; they do not need to cook through. Drain the potatoes on paper towels.

Wash the eggplants and cut off the tips. Peel strips of skin off, leaving rows of skin, alternating with peeled part. Cut into 1/2-inch slices. Lay slices on a cookie sheet and brush generously with olive oil on both sides. Brown about 5 minutes until lightly browned. Turn and repeat.

Meanwhile, melt butter over medium heat and stir in flour. Stir until it bubbles. Slowly pour in milk, stirring constantly. Bring to a gentle boil and remove from heat. Add cheese and stir.

To assemble the moussaka, use a 9-inch x 13-inch pan. Layer eggplant, potato, meat, potato, eggplant, then sauce. Bake 45 to 60 minutes until top is browned. Allow to rest on a wire rack for 15 to 20 minutes before serving.

Makes 8 servings

Stifado (Beef Stew)

1/4 cup olive oil
2 lbs. beef stew meat
3 cups thinly sliced onions
   (about 3 lbs.)
2 cloves garlic, finely chopped
1 can (6 oz.) tomato paste

1 can (10 1/2 oz.) beef broth
1 cup water
2 tbsp. red wine vinegar
1 tsp. allspice
salt and pepper to taste

In an electric skillet or large frying pan, heat oil over medium-high heat. Add the meat and brown on all sides. Remove meat and set aside. Put onions and garlic in pan and cook until lightly browned. Return meat to pan. Add tomato paste, beef broth, water, vinegar, and spices; mix well. Cover pan and reduce heat to low. Simmer stew about 3 to 4 hours or until the meat is very tender. Stir frequently to keep meat from sticking to the pan. The sauce will become very thick.

Makes 6 servings

Roast Pork

2 1/2-lb. boneless pork loin roast
2 tbsp. fresh lemon juice
4 cloves garlic, minced

2 tsp. dried oregano
2 tsp. dried rosemary
salt and pepper to taste

Preheat oven to 450 °F. In a small bowl, combine the lemon juice, garlic, oregano, and rosemary. Rub this mixture all over the meat and sprinkle with salt and pepper to taste. Place the pork on a rack in a shallow greased pan, fat side up. Insert a meat thermometer and place the meat in the oven. Reduce the heat to 325 °F and cook uncovered for 50 to 70 minutes or until the meat thermometer reads 170 °F. Remove the roast from the oven and let rest 10 minutes before carving.

Makes 6 servings

Baklavá

Pastry
1 lb. phíllo pastry
4 sticks butter, melted
4 cups (1 lb.) pecans or walnuts,
    finely chopped

Syrup
3 cups sugar
2 cups water
rind of one lemon
rind of one orange
1 cinnamon stick

Place 7 sheets of phíllo pastry in a 9-inch x 13-inch pan coated with cooking spray. Brush each sheet with melted butter before adding the next. Butter the top sheet as well. Sprinkle nuts on top of the 7 sheets. Then top nuts with remaining phíllo, again brushing each sheet with melted butter. Place pan in refrigerator for 1/2 hour. Cut pastry into diagonal pieces. Bake for 1 hour in a 325 °F oven.

While pastry is cooking, prepare the syrup. In a small saucepan, combine sugar, water, lemon rind, orange rind, and cinnamon stick. Bring mixture to a boil over medium heat. Reduce heat and simmer 10 minutes. Remove pan from heat. Pour hot syrup over cooled baklavá.

Makes 36 pieces

Greek Coffee

2/3 cup cold water
2 tsp. sugar
2 heaping tsp. Greek coffee (found
    wherever Greek groceries are sold)

In a small enameled saucepan, bring water and sugar to a boil. Remove from heat and stir in the coffee vigorously. Return pan to heat. Coffee will boil almost to the top immediately and have a brown foam on top. Just before it overflows, remove from heat, and tap the sides of the pan with a spoon until foam subsides a bit. Return the pan to heat a second time and allow it to boil almost to the top again. Remove from heat and tap again three times. Return to heat for a third time and allow it to almost overflow again. Quickly remove from heat. With a spoon, carefully distribute the foam evenly into two demitasse cups and then slowly fill the cups, being careful not to disturb the foam on top of each cup. Serve at once.

Makes 2 servings

Amorgos (uh mohr YOHS) a Greek island on the east part of the Cyclades Islands.

avgolémono (av gohl EHM oh noh) traditional New Year's soup.

baklavá (bah klah VAH) a famous Greek pastry made of layers of flaky dough with ground nuts and honey.

Caesarea (kay sah REE uh) a city in ancient Cappadocia in Asia Minor (now Kayseri, Turkey), where St. Basil served as bishop.

Cappadocia (kap uh doh KEE uh) city in Turkey.

Christopsomo (krihs TOP soh moh) "Christ bread," the special bread that is a central part of the Greek Christmas dinner and celebrations.

chrónia pollá (KROH nee yuh POH luh) "Many years!"

coliandra (koh lee AN druh) word for Greek Christmas carols in Macedonia.

Constantinople (kahn stan tih NOH puhl) Byzantine name for the city now called Istanbul in Turkey.

Crete (kreet) a large Greek island in the Mediterranean Sea off the coast of mainland Greece.

Dodecameron (doh duh KAM ur ahn) the twelve days from Christmas to Epiphany.

Drama (DRAH muh) city in the northeastern Greek province of Macedonia.

Hellas (hel AHS) the Greek and official name for Greece.

Hellenes (hel EENZ) the official name of the Greek people.

I Yennisi Sou Christe (ee YEHN ih see soo krihs TAY) "Your Birth, O Christ," the title of a beloved Greek Christmas hymn.

icon (EYE kahn) a sacred picture of a saint or other holy figure.

iconostasis (eye kuh NAHS tuh sihs) screen of icons that separates the nave from the sanctuary in a Greek Orthodox church.

ikonostási (ee kohn uh STAH see) a Greek home altar, which includes icons.

kálanda (KAL uhn duh) Greek Christmas or New Year's carols.

kálanda protochrónias (KAL uhn duh proh toh KROH nee uhs) a New Year's carol.

kalí chroniá (kal EE krohn YAH) "Good Year!"

kalí sarakostí (kal EE sair uh kohs TEE) "Good Lent," a greeting during that season.

kalikántzari (kal ih KAN tzahr ee) mischievous and evil tricksters who make trouble at Christmastime.

kaló (kal OH) to invite or shout.

**kaló poth

arikó** (kal OH poh thuh ree KOH) a wish that the first person who enters your house on New Year's Day brings you good luck.

kandíli (kan DEE lee) a candle made of an enclosed glass holder suspended by a chain with a wick attached to cork floating in olive oil.

Kavala (kah VAH luh) city in the Greek province of Macedonia.

kourabiéthes (koo rah bee EHTH ehs) Christmas butter cookies coated with powdered sugar.

koulourakia (koo loo RAH kyah) Christmas cookies with sesame seeds.

Lesbos (LEHZ vohs) a Greek island in the Aegean Sea.

Limnos (LEEM nohs) a Greek island in the Aegean Sea.

loukoumáthes (loo koo MAH theez) Christmas deep-fried honey puffs.

Macedonia (mak uh DOH nee uh) province in northern Greece.

melomakárona (mehl uh muh KAHR oh nuh) Christmas cookies made with nuts.

Minoan (mihn OH uhn) referring to the culture of ancient Crete.

Monokklisia (moh noh klee SYAH) village in Serres, Macedonia.

Mycenaean (my suh NEE uhn) referring to the culture of Mycenae, an influential ancient Greek city that initiated the Trojan War.

na ta poúme (nah tah POO muh) "May we sing Christmas carols for you?"

Nereid (NIHR ee uhd) in Greek mythology, a sea nymph.

Pantocrator (pan toh KRAY tuhr) Christ the Almighty.

paréa (puhr AY uh) companionship; a group of friends.

Pláka (PLAH kuh) district in Athens near the Acropolis that includes some of the old city marketplace.

Sarakosti (sair uh kohs TEE) Lent, during which people fast.

Serres (SAIR ehs) city in Macedonia.

sfrayítha (sfray YEE thuh) a special seal used to print a religious design on communion bread.

skarkántzalos (skahr KANT zuh lohs) "Christ log," the fire kept burning from Christmas to Epiphany in many Greek homes.

spíti horís Yiánni prokopí then káni (SPEE tee hawr EHS YAN ee proh koh PEE then KAHN ee) "A home without a person named John will not succeed."

tessarakosti (tehs ahr uh KOHS tee) formal, as in a formal feast.

Theophania (thay oh fahn EE yuh) Epiphany; "God appears."

Theotokos (thay oh TOH kohs) Mother of Our Lord.

tsambounes (tzam BOO nuhs) a type of bagpipe.

tzoumàka (tzoo MAH kah) a special tapered stick or cane used by some kálanda carolers to knock on house doors.

Vasilopita (vas ihl oh PEE tuh) "Basil's bread," a special sweet bread with a coin hidden inside that is part of the New Year's celebration, named after St. Basil.

Volakas (voh LAH kuhs) a community in Drama, Macedonia.

xeropháyi (zayr oh FY yuh) a strict fast, or "dry eating."

yia to kalo (yah toh KAH loh) "for luck."

Yianna (yee AHN uh) nickname or informal version of the name John used for girls.

Yianni (yee AHN ee) nickname or informal version of the name John used for boys.

zaharoplàstio (zuh hair uh plas TEE oh) a Greek bakery or pastry shop; coffee shop.

Index

Page numbers in *italic* type refer to illustrations.

Acknowledgments

Cover	©C. Vergas, Ideal Photo; ©Clairy Moustafellou, On Location
2	©Walter Bibikow, The Viesti Collection
6	©A. Kalogeridis, Ideal Photo
9	©Robert Fried
13	©Clairy Moustafellou, On Location
15	©Nigel Bowen-Morris, Travel Ink.; Papstamatiou, Margarei Aperis & Sons, Inc.
16	©V. Lioris, Ideal Photo
18	©Velissarios Voutsas, On Location
19	©Massimo Pizzocaro, On Location
20	©Clairy Moustafellou, On Location
21	©Spyros Catramis, On Location
22	©Clairy Moustafellou, On Location
25	©Clairy Moustafellou, On Location
26	©C. Vergas, Ideal Photo
28	©Robert Fried
29	©Clairy Moustafellou, On Location
30	©Robert Fried; ©Loukas, On Location
31	©Velissarious Voutsas, On Location
32	©Spyros Catramis, On Location
34	©Clairy Moustafellou, On Location
35	©Spyros Catramis, On Location
37	©Clairy Moustafellou, On Location
38	©A. Pappas, Ideal Photo
41	©Velissarios Voutsas, On Location
42	©F. Kyriakoy, Ideal Photo
45	©C. Vergas, Ideal Photo
46	©Clairy Moustefellou, On Location
48	©A. Pappas, Ideal Photo
51	©Clairy Moustafellou, On Location
52	©Robert Fried
55	©Spyros Catramis, On Location
56	©Robert Fried
57	©Liondas Chr., Margarei Apergis & Sons, Inc.
58	©C. Vergas, Ideal Photo
61	©C. Vergas, Ideal Photo
62	©Robert Fried
63	©Velissarios Voutsas, On Location
64	©Velissarios Voutsas, On Location

Craft Illustrations: Eileen Mueller Neill*

All entries marked with an asterisk (*) denote illustrations created exclusively for World Book, Inc.